For Lynne,

SKINT KNEES

Reflections on a Scottish Childhood

Hope you enjoy this glimpse into my Scottish childhood.

by Fay (Hawson) Copland

Happy Reading,
Fay

Cover Photo: Testing the Water at Millport, circa 1946

FriesenPress

Suite 300 – 990 Fort Street
Victoria, BC, Canada V8V 3K2
www.friesenpress.com

Copyright © 2015 by Fay (Hawson) Copland
First Edition — 2015
Editor: Renee Layberry

All rights reserved.

No part of this publication may be reproduced in any form, or by any means, electronic or mechanical, including photocopying, recording, or any information browsing, storage, or retrieval system, without permission in writing from the publisher.

ISBN
978-1-4602-4634-4 (Hardcover)
978-1-4602-4635-1 (Paperback)
978-1-4602-4636-8 (eBook)

1. Biography & Autobiography

Distributed to the trade by The Ingram Book Company

TABLE OF CONTENTS

Foreword .... *v*
Dedication .... *vii*
Acknowledgements .... *ix*
Farewell *1*
Our Tenement Home *3*
The World of Our Neighbourhood *7*
Co-operative Living *11*
Sticky Business *15*
"The Wee Yin" *19*
Togetherness *21*
Good News *25*
A Fresh Chapter *27*
Dad *29*
Hogmanay *33*
Special Delivery *35*
Never a Dull Moment *39*
An End and a Beginning *47*
School Camp *49*
The Great Outdoors *51*
School Days *55*
"I'll See You Sometime" *63*
My Scottish Family Album *65*
Glossary *69*
About the Author *73*

FOREWORD

I enjoyed the best of childhoods. Born into a Scottish family during the Second World War, I was cared for by my young parents, three doting grandparents, and an aunt and uncle or two. Oblivious to the fact that war was making life difficult for the adults in my life, I thrived in the abundant warmth and security of their protection and love.

Rationing did not apply to sharing, compassion, inventiveness or laughter and we indulged lavishly in each of these commodities. Nana made beetroot wine that caused a catastrophe, and she and the neighbour handcrafted Plaster of Paris wall plaques that turned out to be hideous. However, the therapeutic value provided by these kinds of enterprises far outweighed any worth the finished product might have had.

As time bore the war years away, we left the old tenement building that had been my first home and moved into a modern housing scheme.

My new surroundings offered a world of adventure which I embraced wholeheartedly. I played soccer in the cow pasture with the boys, picked brambles in season from the hedgerows along the country road behind the houses, collected manure that delivery horses left on the street, (Nana said it was good for the rhubarb plants) and, in my various, enthusiastic pursuits, skinned my knees daily.

I walked to school with the other children in our neighbourhood, joined Girl Guides at our church, took part in a Coronation street party on June 2nd, 1953, and thoroughly enjoyed life.

In July, 1954, leaving relatives, friends, community, and lifestyle, my family emigrated to Canada.

This collection of anecdotes is the story of my childhood. It is full of memories I cherish to this day, memories I feel compelled to share. So I invite you in to experience some of the essence and sentiment (with generous dollops of humour added) of growing up in wartime and post-war Scotland.

DEDICATION

The place you know first is surely the place you remember best.

Renfrew, Scotland is a small town on the south bank of the River Clyde, west of Glasgow and north of Paisley. Here, I was to learn the love and security of my family circle, make my first friends, explore my surroundings, (both urban and rural) and truly take root. It was where, long ago, I belonged. It was my home ground and is the place to which I feel a strong connection, even now.

My friends, neighbours, and loved ones in Renfrew contributed to making my Scottish childhood the rich experience that I treasure. I dedicate "Skint Knees" in honour of each one of them.

ACKNOWLEDGEMENTS

Family members and dear friends offered their support and encouragement as I laboured to commit "Skint Knees" to paper. They understood my need for time to see this project through; I thank each one for believing in me, for their interest in my writing, for their patience, and for their love.

My neighbour and friend, Mr. Doug McConnell, formatted the photographs that appear throughout this manuscript. Thank you Doug, for being so willing to help and for the time you devoted to this important task. Your expertise is thoroughly appreciated.

Photographer and friend, Mrs. Janet Bollinger, took my author photo. Many thanks Janet, for your camera skills and for your insistence on getting it "just right".

Mr. Bob Nielsen led creative writing classes at McMaster University's Continuing Education Centre while I was a student there. Through his assignments, and subsequent comments, I came to believe that I had a worthwhile story to tell and that the strategies and styles he taught would aid me in this task.

He suggested the title "Skinned Knees" after I used those words in a practice assignment on writing a foreword.

Thank you, Bob. You helped me to unearth not only the writer within, but the confidence to follow my dream of telling this story.

On learning the title I intended to use, my lifelong friend, Elizabeth Easby, reminded me that in our part of Scotland, such battle wounds would be referred to as "skint knees". Many thanks, my friend, for supplying this detail of authenticity.

FAREWELL

In the house, there had been much talking and dreaming about it for months. Our lives would be different—better, even. *We* would be different, too. Our hopes were high. And now, on this July evening, the adventure was starting to unfold, to become a reality.

We had readied ourselves—my mother, my grandmother, my sister, and I—and in our empty house, we awaited the arrival of the taxi. Outside, a small cluster of neighbours gathered on this warm, July evening. Perhaps it would have been less painful had it been raining.

By the time the vehicle arrived, the group outside had become a crowd and they waited for us to emerge. I vividly remember walking the short distance from house to curb. Familiar faces pressed in on every side; childhood friends and their parents stretched out their hands to touch us. They all wished us well as we embarked on a journey that would take us to Canada and to my father, who had travelled on ahead a few weeks earlier.

Already, I felt distinctly separated from those around me. I knew I would never again play out in the long, glorious twilight of a Scottish summer evening with my friends, and wander home reluctantly when parents called us in for the night. Those times were gone. I secretly wished this to be just another ordinary night and that I could stay and play until bedtime.

So taken had I been, up to now, with the promise of our new life, that I had not given any thought to what I would be giving up in exchange for it. Suddenly, it became clear to me that the moment of parting had arrived. How could I get through it? How *would* I get through it?

I tried to force a smile, but the lump in my throat forbade it. These folk knew me to be a bit of a tomboy, so I couldn't let myself break down in front of them. I felt I had to show that I was tough, not bothered in the least. Besides, I could see that my mum and my nana were having difficulty with the situation, and I didn't want to add to their troubles.

I found refuge in a corner of the taxi and watched as my neighbourhood, my hometown, and the world of my childhood disappeared from sight. I was eleven years old.

OUR TENEMENT HOME

Nana heaved her considerable body on top of me as a shattering explosion wrenched us from sleep.

"My Goad, they've hit us," she exclaimed, fear reflecting itself in her panicked tone. "Are ye awright, Hen?"

The sound of broken glass tinkling onto the linoleum-covered floor was followed by my parents' soft, scurrying footsteps as they hurried, barefooted and alarmed, through the long lobby that connected their sleeping quarters with ours...

The bed I shared with Nana was recessed into a wall of what we called the kitchen, a room which served as living room, dining room, and bedroom. I slept against the wall, protected from ever falling out of bed by the safety barrier that was my nana. It was the best place to sleep in a tenement flat, for it was near the fireplace. Although the fire was allowed to burn itself out during the night, enough of its heat would have permeated the iron range that surrounded it to keep the room comfortable for hours.

My parents used the front room as their bedroom, their bed set into the wall in an identical recess to ours. Coal was expensive, so the fireplace in that room was lit only when we had visitors. It was the "good" room, the sitting room. A shiny, black piano graced this space, as did my parents' three-piece living room suite, gifted to them as a wedding present by my dad's parents. A large Persian rug covered most of the floor, occasional chairs filled in the spaces among the larger pieces of furniture, and paintings hung on chains from the picture rail that ran around the walls near the ceiling.

If a pianist happened to be among our guests, the piano would be put to good use, accompanying any volunteer soloists. I clearly remember Nana enjoying the limelight as she trilled out "Dark Loch Nagar" for many a gathering.

My family survived comfortably enough, but our location was a precarious one. Our tenement building stood less than a mile from the River Clyde and its shipyards. For the enemy, this region was a prime target. On several occasions, the entire building had emptied during the night, its tenants fleeing to the safety of nearby shelters when air-raid sirens moaned their ominous warnings. My caregivers slept guardedly.

Mother had recently decorated the walls of our flat using a "stippling" technique that involved applying paint to the walls with a sponge. She turned the scullery, with its single sink and cold water tap, into a studio for preparing her materials and for cleaning up. So proficient had she become in her craft that the neighbours took lessons from her.

"Oh Bessie, yer that guid at it," they would flatter when invited in for a look. "Ye'll mebbe show me how tae dae ma place."

They had become accustomed to the shortages and the ration books. They had made their own blackout curtains. They had learned to live with boarded-up windows, rubble in the streets, and family members gone to war. Living became a kind of game as the country's citizens, more notably and inexplicably the women, challenged the deprivation of the time by becoming innovative and somewhat defiant.

Young ladies "tanned" their legs with a special cream and then, employing a straight eye and an eyebrow pencil, drew a line up the back of each leg to simulate a stocking seam. Damn the war—fashion reigned!

Mothers concocted new recipes without rationed ingredients like butter, sugar, and eggs. Long-forgotten knitting yarn was discovered in the dark recesses of thousands of cupboard shelves and knitted up into socks for the troops or items of clothing for family members.

"Dig for Victory" was a slogan created to encourage Britons to grow their own vegetables through the war years. After all, rain still fell and the sun persisted in shining, war or no war. Anyone who had a few square feet of soil at their disposal planted vegetables of every kind. Neighbours shared their troubles, their ration coupons, and their garden bounty.

"Ah wish ye widnae make a' that mess in the scullery, Mother," pleaded my mum as Nana prepared some donated beetroot for boiling and pickling.

"You're aye the same," retorted Nana. "Can ye no' see whit a boon a' this beetroot is?" And with that, she became creative.

Why not make some beetroot wine from what was left, for the family to enjoy with their meagre rations, she reasoned. Like her compatriots, she was determined that the war was not going to prevent her from introducing a little luxury into our daily living.

She made only enough to fill the crystal decanter, placing it carefully and lovingly into the shallow little cupboard that was built into the end of the sideboard. Someday her family would thank her for her efforts, but they would have to wait. Wine takes time to mature...

By the time Nana had ascertained that I was unharmed, my parents had felt for the light switch. Light flooded the kitchen as the two of us scrambled from our bed and joined Mum and Dad in gaping at the havoc that surrounded us. Burgundy liquid pooled around our bare feet, stained the stippled wall surrounding the sideboard, and dripped from the whitewashed ceiling. Pieces of broken crystal covered the soaked, slippery floor, creating a minefield of sharp slivers.

It was not a German bomb that had caused the nocturnal intrusion. The beetroot wine was the culprit. In its fermenting stage, it had exploded, shattering its container and tearing the door off the shallow little cupboard, built so cunningly, into the end of the sideboard.

"Och well," exclaimed Nana, once she'd recovered enough to regain her ability to speak, "we're a' still kickin', an' tae tell ye the truth, Ah wiz never a' that crazy fur that stipplin' joab anywey."

THE WORLD OF OUR NEIGHBOURHOOD

Our end of the street accommodated a mixture of tenements and single-storey row housing. An air raid shelter stood in one corner of a roughly-paved play area, contradicting a set of swings and a joy-wheel. A short, narrow lane, squeezed between buildings, allowed us access onto the high street. Behind our dwellings, at some distance, lay railway tracks, several huge, open water tanks and the river. We couldn't have been more than four or five years old, and this was our playground. That we were allowed to play outside, unsupervised, astounds me now.

As the sun beamed brightly on a sweet, summer afternoon, a group of us trekked to the water tanks. One particular tank fascinated us, for on its surface, a dead seagull floated. We hung ourselves over the low brick wall that surrounded the tank to peer down into its depths and to get a closer look at the grotesque, bloated creature as it sprawled, saturated, in its death pose, before us.

As the afternoon waned and we'd straggled home, an ominous silence descended upon the neighbourhood. Housewives, normally occupied with teatime preparations at this hour, gathered in clutches outside their respective closes. They spoke in whispers of disbelief, their mouths seeming only to shape the words that they uttered. The sun, which earlier had shone so gloriously, seemed to have taken on a mysterious aura, as if in the witnessing of the horrific event, it had become nauseous. Or was it mocking us? One of the children had not come home. The water tank had claimed another victim.

* * *

No one of our acquaintance owned a motorcar or even knew how to drive—but Mr. Anderson, from across the landing, was a bus driver so he was able to rent a car to take his family on a summer holiday.

On their return, having safely delivered his wife, their sons, and their luggage to their upstairs flat, he prepared to drive off to return the vehicle. Three of us, fascinated that a "motor" had actually stopped at our close, decided we would hang onto the back bumper and run behind it. As it picked up speed, my little legs could not keep up the pace; I was dragged through potholes and puddles, my small hands clinging tenaciously to the bumper. When my screams alerted the driver, he stopped the car and ran to my aid, picking me up and carrying me to my mother. I was scraped on one side, from ankle to hip, but was otherwise unhurt. Mother and Nana cleaned my wounds, put me to bed for the afternoon, and administered to Mr. Anderson the cure-all for shattered nerves—a cup of tea.

(A few years later, on a shopping trip into Glasgow with Mother, Nana, and my sister, I had another heart-stopping escapade. We were travelling by tramcar and as we stood on the tram's open rear deck, waiting to get off, the vehicle halted in busy traffic. Thinking we were at our stop, I stepped down onto the street, only to see the tram trundle ahead with my family still aboard. I sprinted after it, amid all manner of vehicles, until a brave pedestrian scooped me off the roadway and delivered me to safety to wait for my loved ones. Mother was in a state of near-collapse by the time we were reunited. As a child, I was hard on her nerves.)

We had all been warned about the dangers of crossing the high street, a busy thoroughfare used by tramcars and buses, lorries, motorcars, and the occasional horse and cart. There were shops on our side where we could safely spend our pennies and ha'pennies on sweeties, crisps, and cheap novelties. One such place was a newsagent's and tobacconist's shop that carried a variety of sweets which we could buy for a ha'penny or even a farthing. The blended smell of tobacco and firewood comes to me yet when I think of the place. The firewood, sold in bundles of short sticks tied together with string, was used as kindling to start not only the ubiquitous coal fires of the homes in town, but also the fire in the shop's fireplace.

But at Lacey's, across the road, you could sit up at a counter and order a fruit-flavoured drink, which Mr. Lacey would prepare for you. This was the treat we longed for. Temptation beckoned, and more than once I skipped over the cobblestones and tram rails with my pals to taste the forbidden, sweet liquid in the shop that smelled like the tropics. That no one was ever flattened by the traffic was pure good luck.

Huge, bulging, burlap sacks, their tops rolled back to display their contents, stood sentry outside a nearby grocer's shop. They contained little biscuits of all shapes and colours, and since confections were rationed during the war, and for some years afterwards, their appeal was irresistible. My cronies and I, surveying the scene and considering the risks, gathered our courage. Quickly snatching up handfuls, we scampered through the lane to the safety and obscurity of our own back street, where we prepared to savour our bounty. But our first crunch was also our last; they tasted ghastly, especially the black ones. Our crime spree had been thwarted by dog biscuits!

Occasionally, his shouts of "Any old rags; toys for rags," would resound throughout the neighbourhood. That was our cue, as youngsters, to race home seeking donations for the ragman as he accompanied his horse and cart along our street. Once, several of my pals were able to exchange their bundles of rags for red, white, and blue tissue-paper streamers attached, in bunches, to the top of slender sticks. In no time, they joined forces to stampede through the streets, coloured streamers fluttering behind them as they held them aloft. I longed to join in, but alas, Mother failed to produce the required old clothes or linens, so the toy of the day was not to be mine.

Nana couldn't bear my predicament and promptly set to work making streamers from scraps of leftover wallpaper. She conjured up a suitable stick to attach them to and soon I was able to join the run with my friends—though my wallpaper streamers didn't seem to flutter as gaily as the tissue-paper variety.

CO-OPERATIVE LIVING

Laundry facilities in the tenements consisted of a separate wash-house at the rear of the property, in close proximity to a drying green. An unwritten timetable for the use of these facilities was to be strictly adhered to, particularly if one valued civility in relationships with one's neighbours. When it was "your turn" in the wash-house, you were in for a period of exertion that would challenge the most rigorous modern-day exercise programme.

Filling the boiler from the only tap—a cold-water one—was your first chore if you happened to have any "whites" to be laundered; "whites" had to be boiled as part of the process in getting them clean. What would the "neebours" think of anybody who didn't boil their "whites"? Getting a fire going in the small space under the boiler would ensure that eventually the water would boil. Each piece of laundry, white or coloured, had to be rubbed with a bar of laundry soap and scrubbed on a washboard in the wash-house's deep sink. Then there was the drudgery of rinsing, wringing and hanging it all out to dry.

The manner in which one hung out one's washing was also subject to the scrutiny of the "neebours". Similar items were to be hung together; socks in pairs, please; shirts, sheets and pillowcases so that they would billow out as they caught the wind. It is unclear who made these laundry rules, but one's reputation as a good housewife depended on strict adherence to them.

If you were lucky, the rain stayed away. More often than not, you would have to snatch your wet washing off the clothesline and bring it indoors to dry on the pulley, a device that hung from the ceiling and worked like a clotheshorse. It kept the laundry items out of the way in the close quarters of a tenement kitchen. That it could be raised and lowered by a rope pulley was, presumably, how it received its name. Our pulley hung over the kitchen table, providing a sort of "ambiance écossaise", especially when festooned with damp laundry.

Keeping the close and stairs clean was the responsibility of the tenement housewives. Residents on the ground floor were responsible for washing the close. Those residing one floor up would clean the stairs up to their level, and so on upwards. This chore was meant to be performed weekly, and anyone who shirked her duties in respect of this task *would* be talked about.

And there were types of closes. Ours was a regular one. Its walls were painted a dark shade part-way up, with a paler version of the same colour from there to the ceiling. A thin accent stripe separated the hues, and they ascended together all the way to the top floor. Ceilings were always whitewashed.

If you happened to live in a building that had tiled walls in the close, you could consider yourself to be "a cut above". The tiles covered the lower portion of the walls and were usually rich in colour, with intricate designs—quite Victorian. Apparently, posh folk lived therein.

The Anderson family had their fireplace rebuilt. No longer was it part of an old-fashioned iron range that you could cook on, like the others in our building, for it had been renovated. Now, it sported a sleek, modern, tiled surface with a new mantelpiece, hearth, and fender. When the fire was lit in it for the first time, the neighbours were invited to come and admire it. Compliment piled upon compliment, one woman providentially topping them all by exclaiming, "You'd actually think the heat was radiating up through the floor."

During the night that followed, we were awakened by the wail of the fire brigade's vehicles arriving at our close mouth.

Indeed, the heat *had* been coming through the floor in Anderson's flat. The wooden joists that supported the floor were smouldering. No one was injured in this episode, but neither did anyone else have their fireplace refurbished.

STICKY BUSINESS

I was enraptured with the shiny red and silver scooter I received for Christmas when I was four. Mostly I rode it indoors, back and forth along the lobby that connected the front and back rooms of our flat. On occasion, one of my parents would carry it down the two flights of stairs to the street so that I could ride it outside. Then I was the envy of the other kids in our tenement, and each one would plead for a "shot" on it. That sleek, gleaming scooter provided us with many an exhilarating ride and did not deserve the fate that befell it one summer day.

Rummaging through the midden at the back of our building, my pals and I came upon a half-empty can of ugly, thick, brown paint, along with some brushes caked with the identical colour. Immediately, the search was on for something, anything, to paint. My gaze fell on the scooter, and I was empowered.

Clots of brown paint glistened on the scooter's surface, on our hands, and our clothing, as well as on the area surrounding us. We hadn't heard of "common element" in the tenements, but our parents would have had to answer to the other residents for our indiscretions. My father, on viewing the violated scooter, seized it and heaved it onto the corrugated metal roof of the back shed. It lay there until the paint dried. I don't recall ever riding it again.

The Nelsons lived next door, and their two sons were often my playmates. One particularly warm day, as our mothers chatted over afternoon tea, we were sent to play outside. Upon discovering that the road tar had become soft, we started scooping it up until each of us had a tennis ball-sized gob of it. As we amused ourselves, rolling it between our hands and forming it into various shapes, it became even softer. Eventually, it stretched between our hands, but would not break its bond. Attempts to free ourselves proved futile. Handcuffed, we stumbled upstairs seeking release from our captor. Our mothers, somehow, knew the remedy: lashings of butter, liberally applied. It freed us in no time, but probably deprived our families of their week's supply, as butter was a rationed substance.

Author with Pals

My dad related a tale about how, as a boy, he'd taken a small ball of tar to school. Fashioning it into the shape of a triangular, liquorice-flavoured, "Victory V" cough pastille, he so convinced himself it was real that he ate it. No one was ever rushed to the hospital over such trivial happenings, and I doubt that Dad even told any adult what he'd swallowed.

***

Children celebrated Hallowe'en by visiting nearby houses, seeking treats. We were always invited in to sing a song, recite a poem, or dance a jig—our choice—in order to earn them. Usual rewards were oranges, apples, and sweeties.

One year, my family hosted a children's Hallowe'en party in our flat. Decorations were scooped-out turnips. Candles lit within them cast a yellow glow through the carved-out shapes of stars and crescent moons. We dooked for apples that floated in a big, square, galvanized tub, getting thoroughly soaked as we tried to snag them. We played a game involving scones, hung by strings and spaced at intervals along the pulley. The scones were liberally spread with treacle, and the trick was to see who could eat the most of their assigned scone without touching it with their hands. It was a sticky, tricky, messy affair, and provided more work for the pulley on wash day.

***

In time, the remarkable day dawned when ration coupons were no longer required to purchase staples and confections. Invited into Mrs. Nelson's flat one afternoon, we were surprised and somewhat stunned when our hostess casually tossed a whole bar of chocolate into each of our laps to enjoy with our tea. It was an act of simple celebration that our dear neighbour wanted to share with those who'd come through the conflict and deprivation with her; she'd undoubtedly emptied her purse to do so.

"THE WEE YIN"

Monday, November 4, 1946 meant nothing to me, for I had not yet turned four, but late that afternoon, my father delivered me to his parents' flat for an overnight stay. I did not understand, nor did I question, the reason for this departure from routine. I remember that my grandma tucked me in for the night and that I lay awake awhile, in a bed that, for my safety, had been pushed against the wall. Taking in the unfamiliar sleeping quarters, I allowed my childish fingers to explore a loose seam in the wallpaper. It felt soothing to strip away the paper, bit by bit, and I picked at it until I had created an unsightly blemish, before drifting off to sleep. I was an "only child" and grandchild at this point, so it didn't matter that I'd spoilt the decor of the guest room. But this hallowed time was about to expire.

When Father reappeared early the next morning, he brought with him the miraculous news that I had a wee sister. There was talk about "the stork" beating on the kitchen window, requesting permission to come in and deliver the little pink bundle it carried in its sling. Dad related how he'd opened the window for the stork, and that is how we got our new baby.

In reality, she had been born, with the assistance of a mid-wife, in the early morning hours of Tuesday, November 5th. She'd already been given the name, Anne, in honour of the grandma who'd cared for me overnight. This happy news delivered, Father didn't linger. He was needed at home on this particular morning. As soon as he departed, Grandma lost no time in getting me ready, and soon we were on our way to see "the wee yin".

A weak, wintry sun struggled through the early-morning fog as the tramcar spilled us out at our destination. As Grandma and I hurried down the narrow lane that led to my home, our steps echoed against the tenement walls, through the still, November air. The grey stone building loomed ahead. Entering the close and ascending to the door with the burnished brass nameplate that proclaimed, not my surname, but my nana's, we stepped into the flat and were welcomed by my father and the warmth of the kitchen fire. (Housing was scarce throughout the war and for several years afterwards. My parents, like thousands of other newly-weds, had taken up residence at a parent's home when they married.)

Daddy quickly escorted us to Mum's bedside. A yellow basket rested beside her on the bed. We called it a "Moses" basket, and I recalled that I had watched my mother giving it a new coat of paint not long ago. My dad lifted me up to see my baby sister nestled inside. Across the room, the grandmothers held a lively, happy conference about her.

My granddad's brown wooden toolbox, now painted in the same yellow tint as the basket, stood at the end of the bed. It had recently been retired to a softer occupation, as a trunk for the new baby's clothes and bedding. Something, I did not understand exactly what, motivated me to climb onto it and offer my rendition of the Highland Fling, but my elders were oblivious to the dance. They seemed somewhat preoccupied.

TOGETHERNESS

My first holidays were spent at Millport, a small town on the Isle of Cumbrae in the Firth of Clyde. It was a favourite destination for the Hawson side of my family and, together, we shared holiday accommodations in a huge house with a view over the beach. My dad's Auntie Bella was never able to live down an event that highlighted a deep-seated fear of hers. In the middle of one night, as thunder crashed and lightning crackled over Millport's bay, fright overcame her; she sought refuge by sprinting to my parents' bedroom and diving into bed beside them.

A necessary part of any British child's holiday in the 40s and 50s was shopping for a new pail and spade to use on the beach. These were items which children dreamed about for weeks beforehand and were available at most of the shops along the waterfront. It seemed necessary to purchase them immediately upon arrival at any holiday destination.

Author, age 3, at Millport

For several days, one summer, my brand new beach toys lay unused. Rain was the reason and I was becoming disenchanted with this whole turn of events. My nana's friend was visiting us, and the two of them, sympathetic to my longing to play in the sand and ingenious in their thinking, hiked to the beach. Managing to stagger back under the weight of a wooden box full of the wet, golden treasure, they dumped it triumphantly into the empty hearth. I spent a splendid afternoon building sand castles in the fireplace of our rented premises.

A feature of the waterfront at Millport, to this day, is its Crocodile Rock. Simply a craggy chunk of stone that resembles the head and upper torso of a crocodile, it's had its facial features highlighted in red and white paint since Victorian times. Each year, the teeth, eyes, tongue, mouth, and nostrils are refreshed with a new coat of paint. It has attracted multitudes of holidaymakers, throughout the generations, who've clambered onto it to have their photographs taken.

Author with Mother on Crocodile Rock

    In the summer of 1947, I was to be train-bearer at my aunt's wedding. Mrs. Lamont stitched together my aqua-coloured, taffeta dress. She was a neighbour and I was obliged to visit her house for fittings. Called away from play, I was never pleased. To my mother's chagrin, I was not the kind of child to get excited about pretty dresses. Mother fashioned my headpiece from a section of her own wedding veil, dyed it aqua, and added a circle of artificial pink rosebuds and some ribbons.

On the big day, I travelled alone in a taxi to my grandparents' house where the rest of the bride's party was gathered. I cannot remember if I had been warned not to crush the taffeta or if I simply wanted to be able to see out of the windows, but I stood in the back of the taxi throughout the trip across town. As we pulled up at my grandparents' close, neighbours, waiting to see the bride, peered into the car to admire me in my finery.

Letting a four-year-old travel alone in a taxi, and with no child car seat, would be considered irresponsible today, but my parents never gave it a second thought. Besides, car seats for children were decades away from being invented and we rarely had the privilege of riding in an automobile. We lived in a small town where everyone knew everyone else. We had just come through a war together and it was an innocent, safe time on the home front.

Aunt Isa and the man she married that day, my Uncle John, played a huge and loving part in my life as a child. Many years later, they travelled to Canada to attend my wedding. I cherish the memories of them.

GOOD NEWS

A letter arrived one day that filled my mother with unbridled joy. The good news was that we would be flitting. My parents had applied for a council house soon after they married, and six years later, they were still waiting. The morning mail brought the news that we had been approved, by the town council, to take up residence in a brand new bungalow, one of sixty-three identical, prefabricated homes being erected in a new part of the town. Putting in the hours until my dad got home must have seemed a penance for Mother but, without a phone, there was no way to reach him at work. She had to contain herself until evening to share the letter's long-awaited message.

We watched as the "prefabs" materialized, especially number 56, which was to be ours. Released to the tenants, these bungalows were still in quite a raw state, and much work was required to make them habitable. One Saturday, I accompanied Dad, Grandpa, and Uncle John to a session of laying linoleum in all the rooms. My dad, a draftsman to trade, was an expert at measuring and cutting the flooring to the exact shape required for each area so that the task was completed quickly and professionally. There were many others to be undertaken to make the house ready, but they could wait until after we'd moved in.

Then there was the matter of the flitting.

On a fresh, spring morning in 1948, two horses, pulling a flatbed cart, arrived early at our close mouth. With our furniture transferred onto it and secured with ropes, the driver ordered the horses underway; they were off to plod the couple of miles to our new place.

I remember my mother's annoyance at the unpacking, because her prized wooden wardrobe had sustained a rope burn across its highly-polished door. Everything else, however, arrived unscathed.

How would Nana feel now that we'd vacated her abode? She didn't have a chance to miss us or to become lonely, for now it was time for her to move in with us. She remained a beloved presence in our home for the rest of her life.

Our Beloved Nana Vernal, on Holiday with Us in Arbroath

A FRESH CHAPTER

Most of the families in our prefab housing scheme consisted of young couples with one or two children each. Many of the adults knew one another from their school days, spent in the older part of town. Some of them were related. They were thrilled to have, at last, "their own door" as they put it, in reference to living in a detached house. It was a step up from sharing a tenement building.

The prefabs provided state-of-the-art facilities for their time. They even had fridges, although ours never worked properly. During construction, a section of one prefab had fallen off the truck as it was being transported; Mother always maintained that it must have been ours because of the faulty fridge.

The ground surrounding our new homes was rough and untamed. Carving lawns and gardens out of this wilderness, where giant rocks and mammoth weeds owned the land, would be a brutal undertaking.

Our youthful fathers launched themselves into the task, discovering and unearthing boulders, tree roots and construction materials as their spades sliced through the soil. With the land cleared, some families chose to plant POTATOES! By summer's end, tall potato plants swayed in the breeze in places where you'd expect lawns and flower gardens. Were these amateur landscapers lacking in creativity or what? I was to learn that, as potatoes grow, they break up the soil, making it easier to cultivate the following year. Into the bargain, those families had a harvest of fine "totties" to last them through the winter.

Throughout that first summer, the children forged friendships with others of similar age, and by the time the new school term began, we had pals to walk with on the way there.

During the following summer, the earth was levelled, raked, and rolled, and grass seed scattered to form tidy front lawns. Backyard drying greens were similarly created to accommodate wet laundry. Flower gardens gradually materialized, bringing forth lupines, gladioli, roses, dahlias, primroses, marigolds, in all their colourful hues.

Our vegetable garden provided potatoes, turnips, cauliflower, Brussels sprouts, beetroot, carrots, onions, cabbage, parsley, and chives. Because Scottish winters are relatively mild, most could be left in the soil and gathered in as needed, throughout the season.

Pea plants yielded bumper crops every summer, but they rarely survived to make it onto the dinner table. We enjoyed eating them raw, and would invite our friends to crouch among the vines and share these garden delicacies, directly from their source.

A clump of rhubarb supplied another free snack. Wrenching stalks of it from the ground, we would plunge one end into our pokes of sugar, "donated" from the kitchen. We were then able to savour the sweet tartness, thus created, as we chewed through the crunchy, gritty treat.

Several small bushes produced red and black currants which Nana harvested to provide us with homemade jam.

Father recycled a pair of old oak bed ends, one becoming our front gate and the other a stylish back for a garden bench.

The wilderness had been tamed!

DAD

Throughout our childhood, Dad was a referee and linesman with the Scottish Football Association. Each week, he would carry his freshly-laundered uniform to his Saturday match in a small suitcase but on his return trip, he carried extra baggage. Packed into that same case, among his sweaty game clothes and muddy boots, would be apples or tangerines or maybe pears, one for each of us to enjoy that evening. I believe this was his way of making up for being absent from his family so frequently.

Once, when he travelled to Ireland to referee at a Schoolboy International Tournament, he brought home a tennis racquet for me and one for the wee yin; on another such occasion, we received small golf putters.

Irish Tennis Racquets

When it came time for Dad to clean his boots for the next match, I would watch, entranced. As he scraped around each leather boot stud to remove the mud, the dried clumps would fall onto a newspaper which he'd spread out on the kitchen table. He approached this task as he did everything, methodically and thoroughly, giving his footwear a finishing shine with Dubbin.

I liked to watch him toasting bread, holding a slice at a time over the kitchen fire with a long-handled fork. If the flames scorched it too much, he would scrape it off with a knife, letting the singed crumbs fall onto the hearth. Spread with a minuscule amount of rationed butter, each slice tasted splendid.

* * *

The Boys' Brigade is an organization, founded in Glasgow in 1883. Its aim is to promote decency, independence, and camaraderie in its youthful members; it achieves this by combining Christian values with activities such as semi-military and marching band skills, gymnastics, camping, team sports and charity events. The "BB", as it is commonly called, exists now in at least sixty countries worldwide.

Dad was thoroughly immersed in The Boys' Brigade throughout his young life and was still serving as an officer when I was a child. I used to enjoy wearing his officer's Glengarry cap with its twin black ribbons attached at the back and a small, matching toorie on its top.

Dad and his Siblings, in Uniform

Dad's brother, Alex, was a life-long member. In early 1984, he was honoured to receive an invitation to Queen Elizabeth's garden party at Holyrood House in Edinburgh, as a reward for a lifetime of service to The Boys' Brigade. Sadly, my uncle passed away a few weeks before that occasion. He would have been so proud to represent his beloved BB at such an event as this.

The Lord Chamberlain is
commanded by Her Majesty to invite

Mr. Alexander Hawson

to a Garden Party
at the Palace of Holyroodhouse
on Wednesday, 4th July, 1984 from 4 to 6 p.m.

Morning Dress, Uniform or Lounge Suit

HOGMANAY

A tradition began for my family during the first years in our prefab home. It centred on the Scots' way of celebrating the transition from old year to new.

    A party would take place at our house on this important occasion, never getting underway until the bells in the town's steeples had heralded the birth of the new year. As is the custom on this night, everyone was expected to be under their own roof for "the bells". Neighbours would arrive at our door shortly thereafter.

    It is a Scottish belief that a household will be blessed with good luck if the "first foot" over the doorstep in a new year is that of a dark-haired male. Nana was always relieved if Mr. Pate, our next door neighbour who was blessed with the required traits, was first to knock. She went so far as to show her annoyance if someone else, less appropriately endowed, was first at our door.

    Of course, my sister and I had been sent to bed hours earlier but would often awaken to the sounds of adult voices singing to Mrs. Pate's piano accompaniment. She could play any song requested, and since she didn't own a piano, she enjoyed playing ours at every opportunity. The old, familiar, Scottish songs were the favourites at this revered time on Scots' calendars.

Once, leaving my bed and padding through to the living room, I observed the celebration in progress. Dad, a tea towel draped over his arm, waiter-style, was passing around a tray of fruitcake, shortbread, and glasses of sherry. Neighbours occupied every available chair, using this chance to chat, to laugh and to sing together as they forgot, for awhile, their daily cares and revelled in each other's company. Mother and Nana would have been busy in the kitchen, making tea and preparing plates of pastries and sandwiches to serve later, on the good china.

Before any of this frivolity could take place, however, there was much work to be done to conform to the traditions of a Scottish Hogmanay and New Year.

The house had to be cleaned from top to bottom. The fire in the hearth was allowed to burn itself out well before the midnight hour. Its ashes could then be disposed of, the fireplace cleaned, and a fresh fire laid for the new year. And, on the stroke of midnight, a window or door was opened to let the old year out and the new one in.

Guests came bearing gifts. A lump of coal was a popular choice as it signified that your hearth would never be without fuel in the coming year. "Lang may yer lum reek," is a saying that accompanies this custom. The present of a food item came with a supposed guarantee that your pantry would always contain enough.

SPECIAL DELIVERY

Every prefab came with a coal cellar in the backyard. They were simply broad lengths of corrugated metal bent into the shape of an arch with a back wall bricked in and a door built into the front. We had our coal delivered into a boarded-off section at the far end, and the rest of the floor space was used to store garden tools and bicycles.

Coalmen wore silver-studded leather covers, fitted over their shoulders, to protect themselves from injury on the lumpy burlap bags of coal which they hefted on their backs from coal cart to cellar. Their cart was pulled by a pair of horses. When the horses dropped manure on the road, Nana would send me out with a shovel and bucket to collect it for her rhubarb plants. She was always quick to notice when this precious commodity became available and encouraged me to hurry before someone else scooped up the prize.

A variety of vendors visited our neighbourhood regularly. We bought our milk from The Scottish Farmer, a dairy business that served many parts of the country. The milkman would deliver full bottles to our doorstep and collect the empties left out for him before whirring away to his next customer in his electric van.

Once, I left my tricycle on the road and the horses, belonging to a local dairy, walked over it with their cart. After that, the front wheel on the trike refused to turn. Father went to the dairy to complain but was informed that it was my fault for leaving the item out there in the first place—and it was! We had to pay for the repair.

Anne and Grandpa Hawson on Trike

A fruit and vegetable cart was accompanied by a colourful character who croaked out his list of wares as he led his horse along.

"Eating apps, cooking apps, cauliflower, lettuce and potatoes, the ripe tomats, Scotch tomats," he would yell repeatedly. We couldn't understand why he called them "apps" when he meant "apples"; "tomats" instead of "tomatoes", but that was his lingo and we didn't question it. On one occasion, a neighbour approached him and politely requested some Scotch tomatoes. "Ah've no' got ony the day," was his gruff reply. So his rhyme never varied, regardless of what was, or wasn't, on board his cart.

Izzi Brothers was a local ice cream business with at least one shop in town. Their van enabled them to reach the neighbourhoods further out. It was a familiar sight and sound to those of us in the suburbs. Cranking out its carnival tunes on its approach, it attracted youngsters like a mechanical pied piper. Off we would run, as its first nasally notes reached our eardrums, to badger our parents for threepence for a pokey hat, a local term for an ice cream cone. Fourpence would get you one with raspberry essence poured over it. But we had to act quickly, before the driver moved on. A visit from Izzi Brothers' van created feelings of contentment or disappointment, depending upon parents' responses to our requests. I'm sure our elders regarded it as a disturbance of their peace.

Sometimes Mother bought ice cream treats for our family, particularly if Izzi came around in the evening. On one such occasion, the vendor advised her that she owed him extra for the pokey hats my sister had obtained from him in recent days. More than once, it seemed, the wee yin had ordered a treat for herself and when he'd handed it down to her, it became obvious that she had no money to pay for it. He explained that he couldn't bear to deprive her because her face was so angelic.

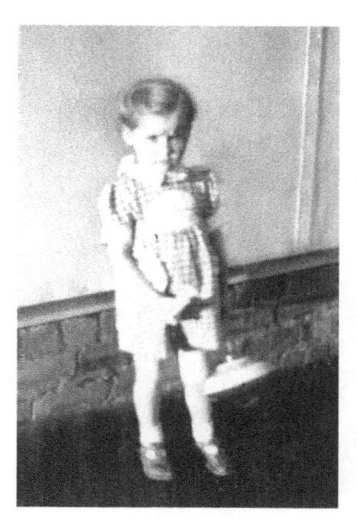

The Wee Yin

In time, Izzi began offering candy treats in addition to the usual vanilla ice cream choices. One such item was a fuchsia-coloured toffee bar that we called "pink stuff".

The wee yin earned herself more than she'd bargained for once for throwing a tantrum when Mother denied her the money for "pink stuff" from Izzi. Her lamenting and thrashing about went on for so long that Mother declared, "Ah'll gie ye pink stuff!" and proceeded to administer a spanking that left the wee yin with a bright pink backside.

One side of the baker's van rolled up like a garage door to display a mouth-watering selection of cakes, tarts, doughnuts, pies, sponges, breads, and rolls. Mothers lined up beside the vehicle, counting their change and deciding what delicacy they might purchase when their turn came. Their children stayed in close proximity or clung onto them, hoping for a special treat for themselves.

Our next door neighbour, Mrs. Pate, invited us in for a meal on the evening we were to depart for our new home in Canada. It became evident, from the appearance of her dining room table, that she had visited the baker's van earlier that day and had bought out a serious proportion of his goods. She provided us with a sumptuous farewell repast, heavy on desserts. I am thankful to her, to this day, for that gesture of kindness to us. God bless her!

NEVER A DULL MOMENT

Our neighbourhood lay adjacent to the airport that served the Glasgow area, so we were accustomed to the sounds of planes as they arrived and departed only a short distance from our homes.

"Wan o' them's gonny come doon aboot us some o' thay days," my mother would often lament, convinced that a crash landing onto our house, in particular, was a distinct possibility—however, no one else ever seemed bothered by the aircraft.

Daylight lingers late during Scottish summers. There was always lots of life on the street during those bonus hours of sunshine. Neighbours chatted over garden fences, children played their various games, the ice cream van's honky-tonk tunes announced its fleeting presence and life was good.

It was on such an evening that the drone of one plane became worrisome. The mammoth craft swept in increasingly lower circles each time it passed overhead. Residents who had been indoors became spectators with the rest of us.

Mother was home alone with us that night and made a quick decision. Dumping the wee yin into the pram and clutching my hand tightly, she headed for Grandma's house where she deemed it would be safer, albeit less than a mile distant.

As we walked, we watched. Suddenly, huge billowing puffs burst from the back of the plane. Some were black; others white. Mother was sure that an explosion was imminent. Then we noticed something remarkable. Suspended from each puff was an airman bailing out of the disabled plane.

The drama in the heavens seemed to cease after that; appearing somewhat less fearful, Mother turned the pram towards home. We had to wait for the morning newspaper to learn the full story.

The military aircraft had been returning from a training mission when its landing gear refused to deploy. As a precaution, the troops were ordered to parachute out and the pilots then managed to slide their flying machine to a safe and unspectacular landing on the runway. At dawn, from our kitchen window, we viewed the crippled plane and were thankful that the incident had ended so fortunately.

* * *

Located beside the airport was a dairy farm run by three spinster sisters whose cattle grazed in a field behind our houses. Jan was the sister we knew best, for she led their animals to the pasture each morning and returned to take them back to the barn at the end of the day. She bossed those beasts like a sergeant major; rarely did they give her trouble as she manoeuvred the herd through the town streets, wielding a sturdy stick to keep them in line.

They were confined to the barn all winter, and on first being released into the field in the spring, they would fairly skip and prance about in a kind of joyful frenzy at being in the outdoors and having space in which to frolic.

If our mothers ran out of milk before the milkman's return, we would be sent over to the farm with a jug and some coins to buy enough to last us through until morning. We approached this errand with apprehension as the sisters were stern in their approach to us. We would summon their attention by knocking on the farmhouse door, whereupon one of them would go to the milkhouse and fill our container with the fresh, frothy liquid. Getting it home without spilling it was another task in itself.

In the summer of 1952, our family holidayed in Newcastle, County Down, Northern Ireland. I can still recall the anticipatory excitement that surged through us, as children, on first sighting the sea and sniffing the salty air on approaching any holiday spot on the coast. The waterfront at Newcastle did not disappoint, for it was magnificent. Many hours we spent wading in the Irish Sea and building sandcastles on the beach, the Mourne Mountains providing a spectacular backdrop.

Sombreros in Ireland, 1952

Adjacent to the beach was a bandstand type of stage where a troupe of entertainers put on a Punch and Judy puppet show twice daily. The wee yin and I attended so often that by the time our holiday ended, we had memorized the entire script.

Back home, with the help of my friend, Marion, we organized our own Punch and Judy show in the backyard. Turning the garden bench around, we converted it into a puppet theatre by draping blankets over its back and using the seat to kneel on as we manipulated our collection of dolls behind the blanket screen. After a few rehearsals, we felt ready to put on the show for other children.

They lined up at our front gate, paid a penny admission and were escorted into our backyard theatre to sit on the grass in front of the "stage". We ran the show for four days, and on the fifth, held a Punch and Judy picnic.

Our audience members' parents donated food items and drinks, and we used the admission pennies to purchase other treats. Waving homemade paper flags and toting the picnic supplies, we paraded, singing as we marched, to the local football park for our day out.

Using our own ingenuity, combined with a generous helping of volunteerism and co-operation from many mums and dads, we not only kept ourselves busy for an entire week during the school holidays, but also managed to capture the collective imagination of the younger prefabbers; no one among us was ever heard to utter the words, "I'm bored". We had no idea what boredom was.

***

Mother would often entertain us with stories of the various animals she'd owned as a child. Apart from a couple of goldfish, we'd never had a pet and, in time, we longed for a creature with which we could interact. Convinced that such an acquisition for our family might be a good idea, she took us, by bus, to a pet shop in Paisley, one day after school. Once there, we were able to browse the variety of options, eventually deciding on two tortoises.

While ringing up the sale, the shopkeeper casually popped each one into a paper bag and twisted the tops shut. Mother was horrified and, refusing to take them from him like that, insisted on a box. Rummaging in the back of the shop, he managed to produce a shoebox. After placing the creatures inside and punching a scattering of holes in the cardboard lid, he handed over our purchases. We could not have been more excited had it been Christmas and our birthdays all rolled into one.

Back in Renfrew, we got off the bus at the stop near the butcher shop where Uncle John worked. Carefully carrying our precious cargo, we decided to allow him the honour of being the first to view the inhabitants of the shoebox.

Hearing our excited voices, he appeared from behind the high, glass counter wearing his navy and white striped butcher's apron and smelling of animal fat. Our uncle had come from a family that was accustomed to having a variety of animals in the household so, not surprisingly, he was enchanted by the tortoises and offered us a few pointers about their care. Father, we knew, would be less receptive.

Paddy and Toby lived in a hutch in the backyard in summer and hibernated in a straw-filled box in our bedroom cupboard all winter.

We allowed them out to wander in the garden each fine day and fed them mostly vegetable leaves. We enjoyed hand-feeding them, watching as their tiny mouths cut out a triangular shape in the leaves with each bite. Neighbours' children found them fascinating. We were pleased that they were interested in our pets and proud to be able to show them off.

Author with Pets

Nana let them out of their hutch one Friday, while we were at school, and promptly forgot about them. Toby was found very quickly, as he had not gone far, but Paddy was nowhere to be seen and was missing all night and into the next day. He was mine, and I was sick with worry.

I was obliged to attend my Saturday piano lesson in spite of my loss. That musical session contributed nothing to my skill at the keyboard, for my thoughts were elsewhere. I kept an eye on the ground all the way there and back, but to no avail. That afternoon, the search widened, and I was to discover him plodding along at the side of the country lane that ran behind our houses. Relief and gratitude flooded over me at having rescued him from an unimaginable fate, and he was none the worse for his overnight adventure.

Author at the Keyboard

Mother enjoyed dressmaking, no more so than when she was creating pretty items of clothing for her two daughters. I detested having to stand still for fittings and protested on each occasion. Once, though, I was so desperate for a particular piece of clothing that I stood beside Mother the entire time she spent at the sewing machine. Fittings were no problem for me during this project.

She had decided to recycle our wartime blackout curtains to make overalls for my sister and me. The material was actually dark brown and, stitched together with white thread, they made stylish playclothes. When my friend, Marion, saw them, she immediately wanted a pair. Mother agreed to make them for her, out of her family's blackout curtains, which really *were* black. She used red thread for this pair. We thought ourselves to be quite special when we appeared on the street wearing these "hot off the presses" fashion statements.

* * *

Aunt Isa was a member of Girl Guides at our church throughout her youth and had become a lieutenant in the organization as a young adult. Having no children of her own, she took great interest in the lives of her only two nieces and the activities we enjoyed. When I became old enough, much to her delight, I joined The Guides, along with Marion.

Regular inspection was carried out weekly, which meant that we would not have thought of turning up at a Girl Guide meeting without being scrubbed clean and properly attired in well-pressed uniforms and sporting shiny shoes and tie badges.

Author in Uniform

If we had any spending money, the two of us liked to visit Trento's fish and chip shop after our meetings, where we would each purchase a poke of chips to eat on the way home. And we walked home in the dark by ourselves!

We were involved in church parades, alongside the Brownies, Lifeboys, and Boys' Brigade ranks, marching to the music of the BB bugle band, complete with drum accompaniment.

We sailed down the Clyde to Rothesay one summer day, where we cooked a meal over a campfire on the beach. It was here I learned, during clean-up, that a handful of wet sand makes a good pot scrubber in the absence of the real thing.

AN END AND A BEGINNING

Occasionally, when the weather turned threatening during morning school hours, we would be kept in class throughout our regular lunch hour and sent home earlier than usual in the afternoon. When we were released early and unexpectedly on February 6th, 1952, inclement weather was not the cause.

News of the death of King George VI had filtered northward to Scotland and we were informed in school. Radio was the default source of information until the evening newspapers hit the streets. If those at home or in the workplace didn't happen to be tuned in, they wouldn't know until, by word of mouth from those who'd heard, the sombre message spread. The sad reality seeped slowly into every corner of the United Kingdom and over her populace, leaving her citizens stunned and unbelieving. The BBC cancelled all regular programming and substituted recordings of gloomy musical selections, with intermittent bulletins about the passing of our beloved monarch. A mantle of mourning cast itself over the entire nation.

We returned to school the following morning and were called to an assembly in the gym. I experienced, for the first time, the observation of a minute of silence, in tribute. To restless primary and junior students, a minute really is a considerable amount of time! We struggled with the singing of "God Save the Queen", replacing masculine words with feminine ones, throughout the anthem. It all seemed so strange. It was a concept we'd never lived through and a lesson in how so much can change in a heartbeat—or in the sudden absence of one.

Sixteen months later, a very different mood permeated the nation.

On the morning of June 2, 1953, a stream of friends and neighbours began arriving at our home, jamming themselves into our tiny living room. Even when all the seating had been occupied, they continued to come, squeezing in wherever they could find a space to sit on the floor. The attraction was our family's recently-purchased television set on which we were preparing to watch the coronation of our new queen. It did not seem to matter that our TV showed only black and white pictures on its 12-inch screen—we were captivated by the spectacle unfolding in London.

Over the intervening months, from the passing of the king to the crowning of his daughter as queen, two women in our prefab community took it upon themselves to visit all the homes regularly, collecting funds to put on a coronation street party.

When the ceremony ended, our audience dispersed to ready themselves for the outdoor celebration. My father manned the microphone during an afternoon of games and races, geared to every age group; there were even events for our parents who surprised and amazed us with their youthful athletic abilities.

Long tables were set up at one end of our street so that everyone could sit down together for the celebratory meal. I do not remember what was served, but it would have been a summer repast. I know it was topped off with a huge cake, into which a small girl, seated near me, plunged her finger for a preview sample of the icing. Each child received a souvenir mug, filled with treats, as a keepsake of this remarkable day in history. And the rain stayed away!

SCHOOL CAMP

Early on the morning after Coronation Day, my chums and I were to embark on a splendid adventure. This was the year our school had been given the opportunity to send its ten-year-olds, for two weeks, to a camp near Edinburgh. Struggling along the platform of the Renfrew station with our suitcases, we boarded a train and waved good-bye to our parents. Along with our teachers, we travelled to Edinburgh, and from there, by bus, to Middleton Camp, a few miles outside the capital city.

As it was a school camp, we were obliged to attend classes while there. The classrooms were individual ones, probably portable, and here, we finished out the school year curriculum in an idyllic country setting. Art classes were held round the lily pond on the property; walks in the woods became science lessons that allowed us to study wildflowers, plants, and trees in their natural environment. We were to enjoy an excursion, on one of the days, to Edinburgh Zoo. There, for the first time, I encountered an orangutan and was thoroughly frightened by its big, sunken face, fringed with brownish-orange hair that stuck out at all angles.

We were housed in long wooden dormitories named after members of the royal family. The girls slept in the Princess Elizabeth and Princess Margaret dorms on one side of the big, grassy common. Boys were allocated to Prince Philip or Prince Charles sleeping quarters, across the common. That the sleeping arrangements included bunk beds filled us with glee. A small bedroom at either end of each dormitory gave our teachers a measure of privacy.

One building on the property housed the tuck shop. With some of my spending money, I bought my mother pink plastic salt and pepper shakers and my father, a comb. The rest I spent on candy treats for myself. Rhubarb rock, long sticks of candy, molded and coloured to resemble the real thing, was one of my favourites. Edinburgh rock, shorter pastel-tinted sticks with the consistency of chalk and slightly fruit-flavoured, was also a regular choice of mine.

We would adjourn to the auditorium each evening; here we would partake of, or participate in, various forms of entertainment. We watched movies, had sing-songs and held talent shows. The teachers had the opportunity, one night, to entertain us, and we found ourselves somewhat taken aback at how human they became in this setting. Our own teacher, sporting a pair of shorts, got up on the stage, lit a cigarette, and took a couple of puffs; holding it expertly, (causing us to wonder if she did this regularly) she sang "Woodbine's a Rare Wee Fag" about a particular brand of cigarette. We were both stunned and delighted at her candour.

The time we spent at this magical place introduced us to a world of coping with everyday living, even doing small amounts of washing by hand in the deep sinks of the camp laundry room and hanging our garments to dry on the clotheslines provided.

We were empowered with this freedom of being in charge of ourselves; it felt good. It was, in a way, a turning point in our young lives. Our teenage years were still a good way off, but we had been given a foretaste of what was to come—and it was glorious.

THE GREAT OUTDOORS

Along one side of the country lane behind our houses, bramble bushes grew in abundance. In summer, the brambles turned from green to red and then to a glistening black as they ripened. The black stage meant they were ready to eat. Usually, though, we couldn't wait for the fruit to ripen; we picked and ate the green and red berries, bringing on many an upset stomach and a vow never to do this again, ever! Our lack of patience for the ripening meant that there were not many berries that survived to maturity. One summer, I did managed to pick a full jar of ripe ones for Nana to turn into jam, a free gift of nature's bounty from our own back lane.

Below the bramble bushes, the undergrowth held hazards that caused us grief from time to time. Jaggy nettles would tear at our legs as we plunged in to get at the best brambles. The pain was instant but, fortunately, fleeting. Other nettles inflicted a more lasting misery. Their large, lush, lovely leaves looked innocent enough, but the fine hairs on their surface would raise itchy welts on the skin if you as much as brushed against them. Luckily, nature provided a leafy antidote, even arranging for it to grow in close proximity to these lurking menaces. Docken plants flourished in abundance alongside the stinging nettles, and instant relief could be secured by rubbing their juicy leaves against the torturous rash. So much we learned about the natural world by simply having the freedom to play and explore in the outdoors.

Opposite the hedgerows, where the brambles grew, were enclosures in which townsfolk kept hens. We were fascinated by the birds and enjoyed watching them as they ran to peck up the chunks of bread we often brought to feed them.

One summer evening, my friends and I found the severed foot of a hen in the lane; we entertained ourselves by taking turns pulling on the exposed ends of the tendons to cause the gory extremity to clutch, grasp, open and close—a "hands-on" educational experience, but grotesque all the same.

At the end of the lane lay the King George V playing fields, the site of our Punch and Judy picnic. Several football pitches and a cycle track were laid out within its confines, as well as a pavilion which housed showers and change rooms for competing teams. It was a vast, grassy playground, popular with the neighbourhood children, particularly on quiet days when no organized events were scheduled. A rather grand veranda stretched across the front of the pavilion, widening out at each end into a circular space. These end spaces became perfect "apartments" for Marion and me as we occupied ourselves with our doll families, playing undisturbed for long periods of time.

We had observed how cyclists whizzed around the cinder track, like hounds after a rabbit. It looked so easy and so inviting. We would bring our bikes and zoom around like that! We learned a greater appreciation for those we'd watched as we crunched along in slow motion through the cinders, barely able to gain enough momentum to keep our bikes upright.

Two small bungalows, one on each side of the pavilion, housed the groundskeepers and their families. We discovered that one of the families stored the supply of soft drinks and biscuits meant to be sold at the pavilion when an organized game was scheduled. If we happened to have a few pennies, we could knock on their door, and they would allow us to purchase a biscuit or a bottle of "ginger" from them.

But the main attraction at the playing fields was its drinking fountain. Here we could have a drink for free, and the source was unlimited. The wee yin washed a neighbour boy's maroon school sweater in the fountain, and both she and the sweater's owner returned home, their clothing blotched with red dye. His mother was not at all amused.

Many of the friendships, made in those years, remain intact today, in spite of the fact that numerous prefabbers are scattered across the globe in the far-flung places their lives have taken them. If you were to ask any one of them about their childhood, I believe the answer would reflect unbridled enthusiasm for, and fond recollections of, the community of "wee hooses" which gathered us in and held us in its embrace for a time.

Our Gang

Young Prefabbers

SCHOOL DAYS

My formal education began in an ancient building in the old part of town. Named Blythswood Testimonial, it was the school Mother had attended.

We used sand trays when learning to form the letters of the alphabet. Carefully shuffling the dry sand until it was evenly distributed in the tray, we then used an index finger to trace, repeatedly, the letter of the day.

The Second World War had just ended and there were still shortages of all manner of everyday items. I can only guess that school supplies were among them, because we were required to erase former pupils' work in order to create clean pages to print on. After six months at Blythswood, I transferred to Moorpark Public School when we moved to our new home. It was where my father and his siblings had spent their early school days. I attended for five years, until we emigrated.

Moorpark was not as old as Blythswood and consisted of two buildings, aptly named "the wee school" and "the big school" by their clientele. These names denoted, not only the size of the structures, but also the size of the pupils who filled them.

A huge expanse of empty ground lay beside the school buildings. Only a few clumps of grass managed to survive here, for it was a well-worn space, its dirt surface packed solid by the feet of droves of schoolchildren and other local inhabitants travelling over it for generations.

We rarely share our style of imagining but, in my young mind, all the stories in the Bible played out on that same piece of waste ground. Perhaps it was due to receiving so much religious instruction in our classrooms nearby that caused me to make such a connection. Each morning, we listened as our teacher shared a story from The Bible. We then sang two or three hymns and, at times, were required to memorize the more familiar passages such as The Ten Commandments and The Beatitudes. I would guess that we were exposed to at least as much Christian education in our classrooms as we were at Church or Sunday School.

In reality, this open space was the location of a carnival that would arrive periodically. We called it "the shows". The show families lived in caravans on site and their children would be registered, for the duration of their visit, in our school. We came to know them as they returned time and again. These families travelled widely throughout Scotland, causing us to wonder how their children coped with the fragmented style of education that was their lot.

Dad was not particularly enthused about the shows but he agreed to accompany us one evening. I can be truly certain that Mother gave him strict instructions about watching over us in such an environment. He took us on the dodg'ems and when we received a hard hit from another car, the wee yin smacked her head on the dashboard. Instantly, a huge lump appeared on her forehead. Dad must have been cringing at the thought of taking her home in that condition. Of course, Mother was furious at him. She could not believe that he would think it was fine to take a two-year-old on such a ride.

The schoolyard, ringed by wrought-iron railings that stretched to the sky, was completely paved in cement, and tall iron gates stood sentry at the entrance.

A few parents would appear during morning playtime, bringing flasks of hot tea and snacks, which they passed through the railings to their youngsters. The rest of us had to be content with a "play piece" brought from home, in a brown paper bag, to eat at break.

The school toilets were housed in out-buildings that stood on the playground. A roof sheltered the row of toilets but the rest of the facility was open to the sky, so a chilling experience awaited those who requested permission to "leave the room", especially during a Scottish winter.

The janitor's house occupied the middle ground between the two school buildings. He lived there with his family and was always on duty. He was required to wear an official-looking uniform: a dark suit, always worn with a tie, and a hat like one a policeman would wear.

Not a blade of grass existed in this environment but, in spite of its foreboding appearance, we managed to make it an arena of entertainment and sport.

Seasonal activities unfolded on the playground before morning classes, at playtimes, and when we returned from mid-day meals.

Football was the game of choice for boys, except in snowy weather when they would occupy themselves on "slides" they made in the schoolyard. The footfalls of swarms of youngsters created these slides by stamping the snow into slippery runways. A running approach and a launching of oneself onto the glazed surface guaranteed a thrilling ride or a nasty tumble. Trying to stay on one's feet was the challenge. In the British climate, the slides disappeared quickly but while they lasted, they supplied exhilarating exercise and great fun at no cost, except for an occasional skint knee!

Girls made slides too. However, their choices of outdoor games and activities far outnumbered those of their male classmates.

"Whips and Peeries" made for a favourite playground pastime and one was of absolutely no use without the other. A wooden spinning top with a metal tip at its pointy end was paired with a leather thong attached to a wooden handle. By wrapping the thong around it, you could set the peery spinning with a flick of the wrist, or by kneeling on its flat top with one knee and yanking the whip away. An occasional stroke from the whip kept the action going. A peery top, decorated with various colours of chalk, was a thrill to watch as the patterns blended in a pleasing way, the faster it spun. This was a game of dexterity paired with an eye for colourful design.

"Peever" was similar to Hopscotch, except that you were required to nudge a small disk into each box with the side of your foot as you hopped along the mapped-out template that we would chalk onto the surface of the play area. If you were lucky, you owned a disk made of marble. A marble one would slide, oh-so-smoothly and silently, across the ground. For those of us who had to find an alternative, a flat shoe polish tin had to suffice. These second-class peevers tended to rattle and bounce their way along the game grid, making a cheap, tinny noise as they hesitated their way to the finish line. Owners of marble peevers usually won this game.

"Scraps" had their place and their season in the schoolyard too. Made of paper and sold in sheets of multiple images that were attached by tabs to one another, they had to be cut apart. They were cut-out pictures of animals, flowers, angels, children, Christmas and Easter icons, photos of the royal family, etc. We would carry our scraps in a hefty book to keep them flat and separated from one another among the pages. Trading them was how we acquired "sets", different sizes of the same image. We kept the members of a "set" together as if they were a family, and their place between the pages, their home. Pre-war scraps were revered possessions; they could not be bought in shops, only acquired by trading. They were the antiques of the scrapping hobby.

A teacher would appear on the playground to ring a handbell when it was time for classes to begin. At that, all play activities ceased. Gathering up our accessories, we would dash to line up in class groups. Marching music, played on a piano in the main hall (usually by a teacher but often by one of the older students) kept us moving; it seemed to command order among the student battalions.

There was a school uniform, although it was not compulsory that it be worn, since this was a public school. I loved mine and wore it most days, learning to knot my tie very early on. Girls wore a white blouse under a navy tunic, a striped tie in the school colours of gold and navy, knee socks, and sturdy oxfords. Boys wore short, navy or grey trousers with white shirts, but the rest of their outfit matched ours. A blazer, trenchcoat or heavy winter coat (also in navy) was worn, depending on the season. Girls wore bérets, and boys, caps, emblazoned with the school crest.

On Sunday evenings, my mother would tack down the box pleats of our tunics, press them with a hot iron and let them cool down before she removed the stitches, leaving the pleats with fresh, sharp edges. The garments were then hung up in readiness for Monday morning and the week ahead. There was no such thing as "wash and wear" in those days.

The strap was used regularly to control unruly behaviour, inattentiveness, talking in class, and failure to come up with the correct answers. Lacking instant recall of multiplication facts or reading vocabulary was grounds for this punishment; sometimes the whole class would be called out to be recipients of the torturous thong if the teacher had had enough of our shenanigans.

The first time I got the strap, it was for not knowing the word "were" on the class reading chart. I was truly mortified. Any time a teacher had to reprimand me, her words would ring in my ears for days; getting the strap was more of a mental torment than a physical one. I would never share these events with my parents but would carry the shame and hurt until they became distant memories or until my best friend happened to receive the same punishment. Then we were full of bravado and claimed that it didn't hurt a bit.

Some pupils, especially certain boys, got the strap every day, sometimes more than once; one teacher had two straps—a small black one was for lesser offences and a big brown one, for major wrong-doings.

* * *

Because Grandma's house was close to the school, it was arranged that we would eat there during our noon break. Grandma always had dinner ready for us and for almost every working member of the family. Grandpa and our two uncles would arrive, clad in their dungarees and smelling of heavy industry. They all worked in Babcock and Wilcox, a local firm which manufactured industrial boilers. My Aunt Isa even returned on the tram, from her job in Paisley, for this mid-day meal. It was normal for Grandma to cook for six of us; on Mondays, when washday was in progress, her kitchen was extra busy as she juggled her laundry tasks with providing sustenance for all of us. She never sat down for the meal, taking hers after we had all returned to work and school.

It was during these dinnertimes that I first heard of Australia. Grandma's brother, Alex, had emigrated to Sydney in the 1920s, had married, and raised a large family there. Grandma would share with me the thin, blue, pre-folded air letters he sent home to her from time to time. Once, she was the recipient of a fold-out postcard with many views of the city of Sydney, including its famous Harbour Bridge. To this day, whenever I happen to see a picture of that bridge, I think of Grandma's postcard, sent to her by a beloved and missed brother, so long ago.

The Sunday Post newspaper always carried the cartoon adventures of "The Broons", portraying day-to-day living in a large Scottish family and "Oor Wullie", a small lad getting into the predicaments of a typical boyhood. Each story occupied a full page of the paper. It was my Grandma who shared them with me, explaining how to read a comic strip.

Those who couldn't go home or to a relative's at dinnertime partook of the famous British school dinners, which were, in my limited experience, really very good. You would receive a full three-course meal: soup, a main course of meat, potatoes, and vegetables, followed by a dessert (which was often hot custard with stewed apples, prunes, or rhubarb, or baked rice pudding with raisins). It "stuck to our ribs" as our elders would say, warding off the chill of so many damp days during the school year.

Having money to spend on the way to or from school made the journey an adventure in perusing and purchasing treats in the various shops. A penny or two would get you a pink sugar mouse, a lucky dip, a cinnamon stick or a liquorice stick as well as a variety of "sweeties". (Mother related that, in her day, children would light the end of the cinnamon sticks and smoke them, but we were not that inventive or courageous.) Liquorice sticks had the appearance of small, brown twigs; they were, in fact, the roots of the liquorice plant—if you chewed on an end, it became soft, yellow, and stringy as the delicious flavour was released. In one shop, you could buy a brown paper bag full of assorted biscuits for tuppence—a bargain! The catch was that they were broken; adults wouldn't purchase them in that condition, but that didn't matter to us.

On one occasion, every student in our school received a bag containing three or four apples, a gift from Canada to British school children. I don't recall the reason for this windfall, but the crisp, juicy Canadian fruit was welcomed, consumed, and relished. I suppose the apples caused us to think of far-off Canada and the people who arranged this unexpected surprise. For me, it was a foretaste of the future.

"I'LL SEE YOU SOMETIME"

The taxi headed towards Glasgow and the main railway station. We had faced a series of tearful farewells over the previous week, and our last goodbyes were behind us—or so we thought. Unable to bear the final parting, my paternal grandma, along with my auntie and uncle, decided to leave town before our departure, for a holiday in England. When we were able, eventually, to share with them our stories of this life-altering evening, we learned that they had gone to a cinema in their resort town; Grandma and Auntie, whose thoughts were of us, had wept throughout the entire film.

But my dad's young bachelor brother, Alex, had not gone with them. He turned up at the station and was able to come aboard the train to see us settled for the trip south. I remember Uncle Alex's last words to us: "I'll see you sometime." It was hard, this emigrating. Years would pass before we saw him or our other loved ones again.

Next morning, we boarded the Cunard liner, Scythia, at Southampton. As she set sail, bound for Quebec City, we gathered with other passengers on deck. People waved to each other from ship and shore. Mother surprised me by joining in.

"Why are you waving?" I inquired. "We don't know any of them." To my way of thinking, there was no point if no one we knew was there to see us off.

"Wave anyway," she replied, her gaze fixed, not on me, but on the receding British coastline.

Instantly grasping her reasoning, I joined Mother in bidding a silent farewell to all that we'd known of the comfortable world that was home.

- The End -

MY SCOTTISH FAMILY ALBUM

Author with Father

Grandma Hawson with Us, 1947

Hawson Family at a Wedding

Author with Father, 1943

Author with Father

Grandma and Grandpa Hawson with Us

Oary Boat Ride with Mom and Dad, Ireland, 1952

GLOSSARY

a'	- all
aboot	- about, around
Ah	- I
Ah'll	- I'll
Ah've	- I've
an'	- and
anywey	- anyway
awright	- alright
aye	- always or yes
caravan	- mobile home
chips	- French fries
close	- hallway entrance to a tenement building
close mouth	- doorless entrance into the close
council house	- rented from town council
crisps	- potato chips

dae	- do
dodg'ems	- bumper cars
dooked	- bobbed (for apples)
doon	- down
dungarees	- overalls
fag	- cigarette
farthing	- 1/4 of a penny
fender	- raised border surrounding the hearth
firth	- the opening of a river into the sea
flitting	- moving house
football	- soccer
fur	-for
gie	- give
ginger	- any kind of carbonated soft drink
Goad	- God
gonny	- going to
guid	- good
ha'pennies	- halfpennies
Hen	- affectionate name for a female, like dear, honey, sweetheart
Hogmanay	- New Year's Eve
hooses	- houses
housing scheme	- subdivision
jaggy nettles	- thistles
joab	- job
joy-wheel	- merry-go-round
kickin'	- alive, living
lang	- long
lobby	- interior hallway
lorries	- trucks

lum	- chimney
ma	- my
mebbe	- maybe
midden	- communal garbage site
motor	- motor car
neebours	- neighbours
no'	- not
o'	- of
och	- oh!
ony	- any
Oor Wullie	- Our Willie
poke	- cone-shaped paper bag
rare	- great, wonderful
reek	- smoke (i.e., a chimney)
scullery	- small room for cleaning, storing kitchen utensils, dishes
shot	- a turn (on a bike, etc.)
skint	- skinned
sweeties	- candies
tae	- to
thay	- they, these
The Broons	- The Browns
the day	- today
The Wee Yin	- The Little One
toorie	- pom-pom
totties	- potatoes
treacle	- molasses
tuppence	- two pennies
wan	- one
whit	- what

widnae	- wouldn't
wiz	- was
ye	- you
ye'll	- you'll
yer	- your, you're

ABOUT THE AUTHOR

After frequent moves around southern Ontario in the early years after immigrating, Fay's family settled in the town of Burlington in 1961. She attended Hamilton Teachers' College and secured her first teaching position in Oakville, situated along the north shore of Lake Ontario. It was there that she taught the primary grades and discovered that children's literature interested her. Maybe someday, she thought, I will write a book for my students.

Married in 1965, Fay and her husband made Oakville their home and remain residents there to this day. They have a daughter and a son who have provided them with four grandchildren. One of their greatest joys is spending time with the little people in their family.

Over the years, Fay has been well-involved in the work of her local United Church. During a congregational trip to Toronto's Metropolitan United Church, she became intrigued by its carillon, which led her to write her first children's book, *Hidden Treasures—A Story of Church Bells*. She hopes to write more books for children, and continues to draw inspiration from the adventures of her grandchildren.

CPSIA information can be obtained
at www.ICGtesting.com
Printed in the USA
BVHW081924240721
612087BV00001B/17